# This Dental

# Coloring

# Book

# Belongs to

______________________

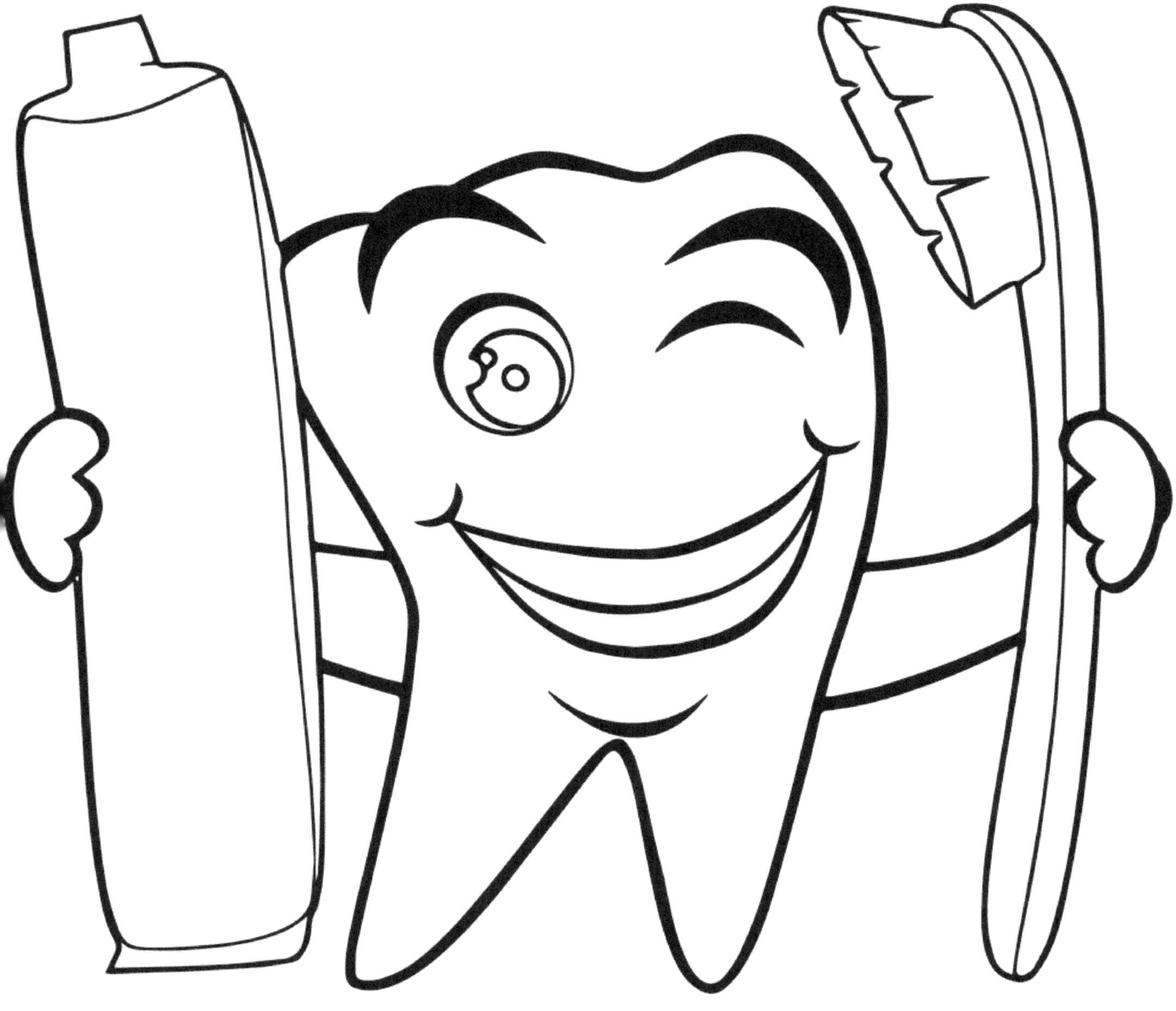

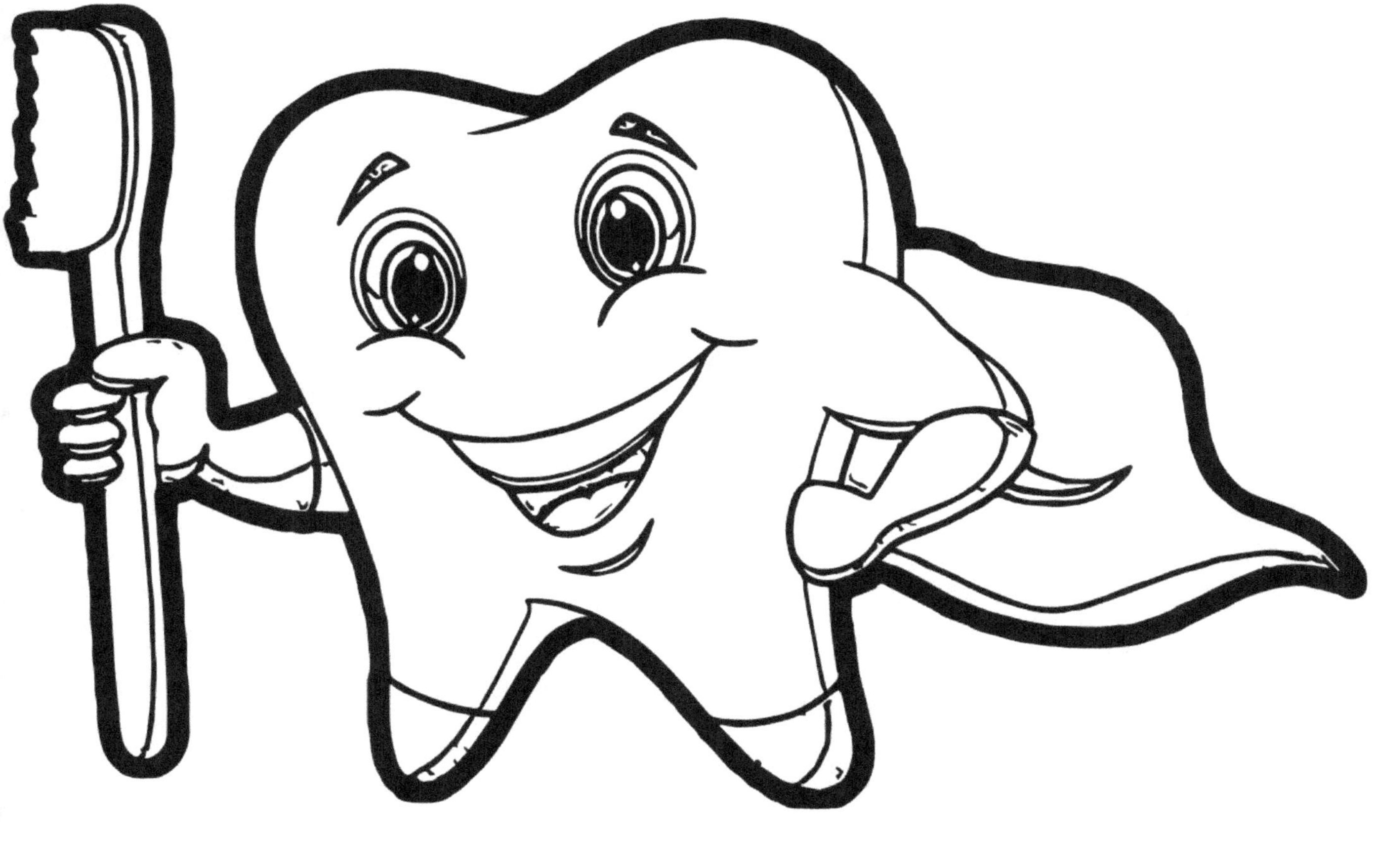

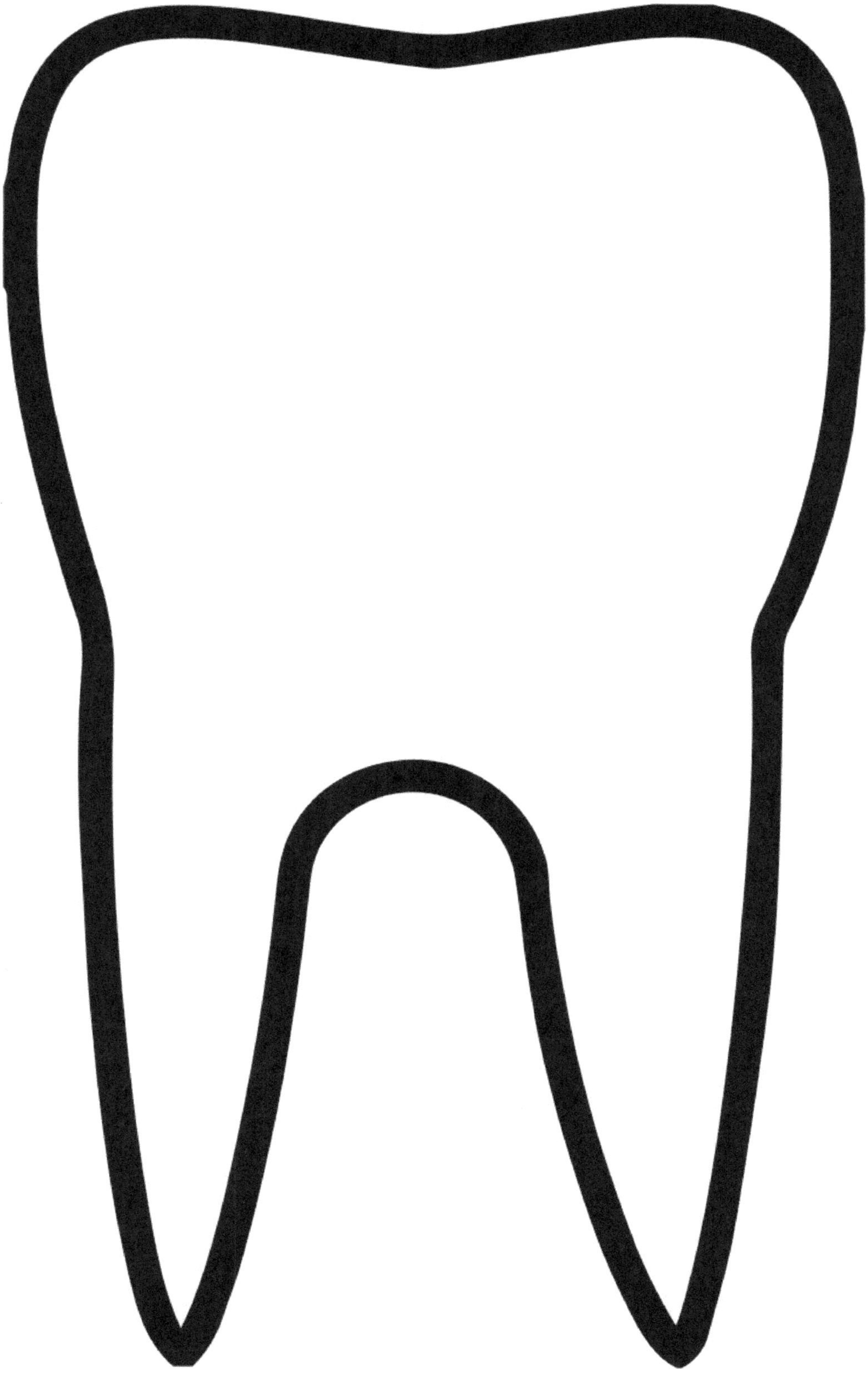

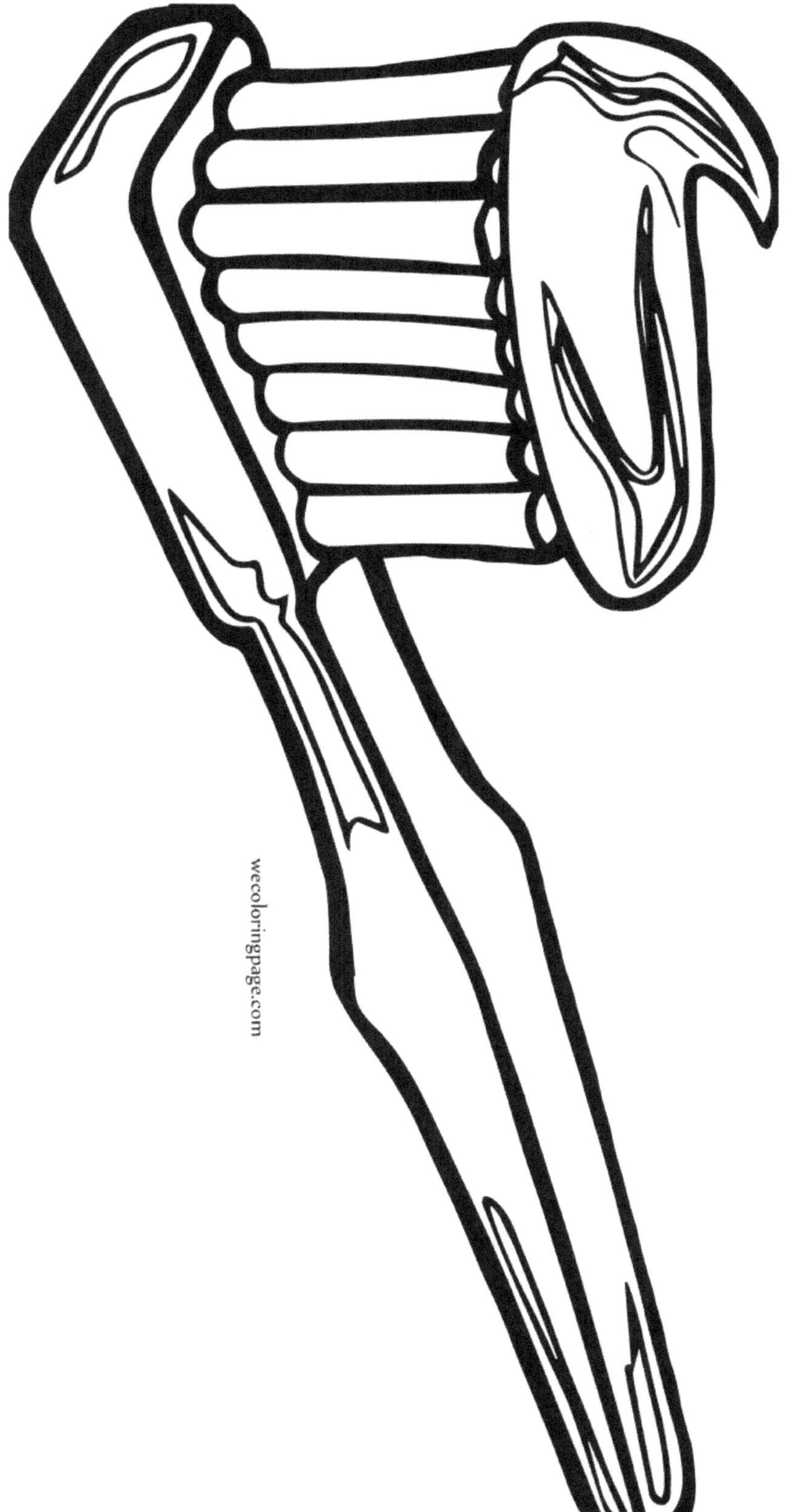

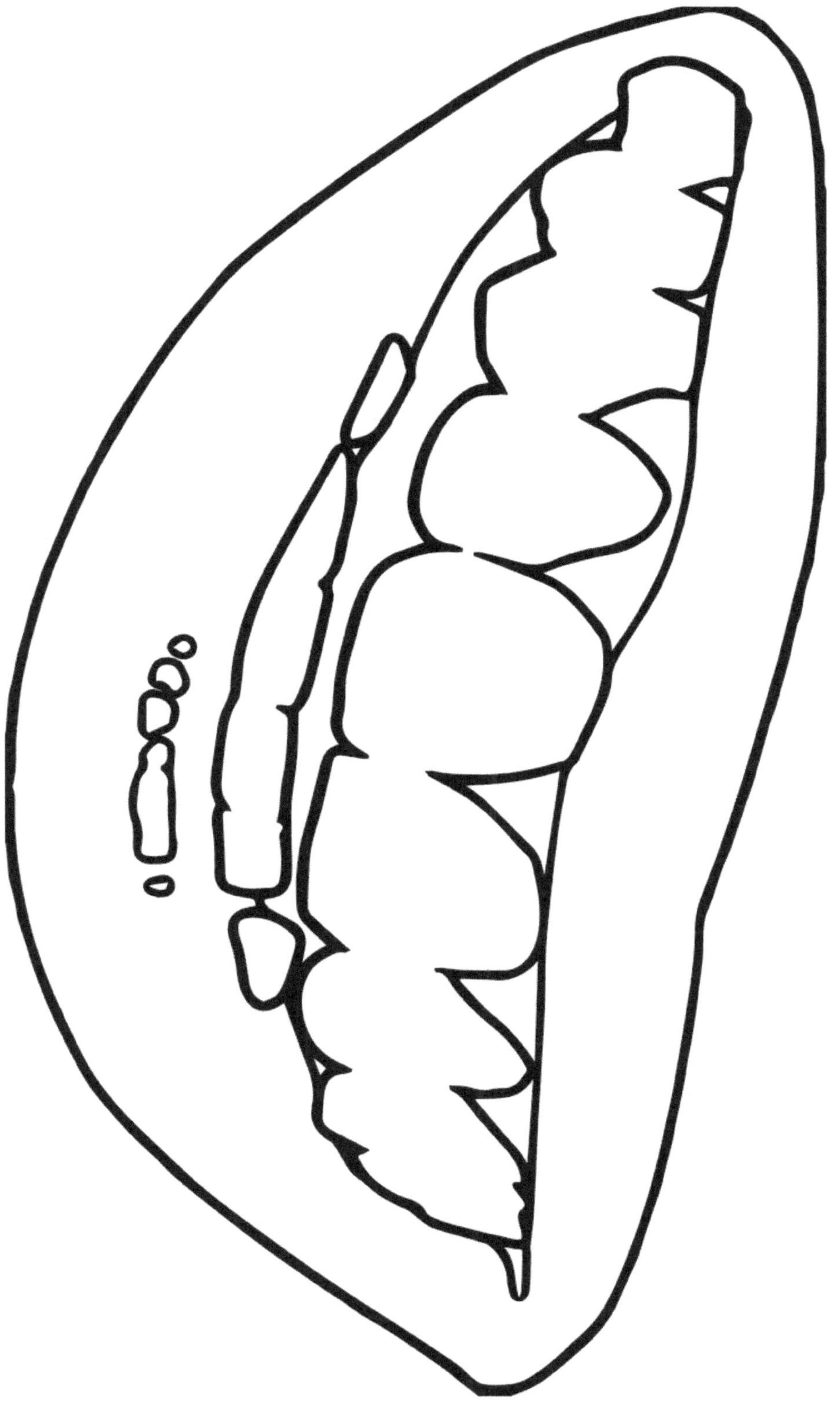

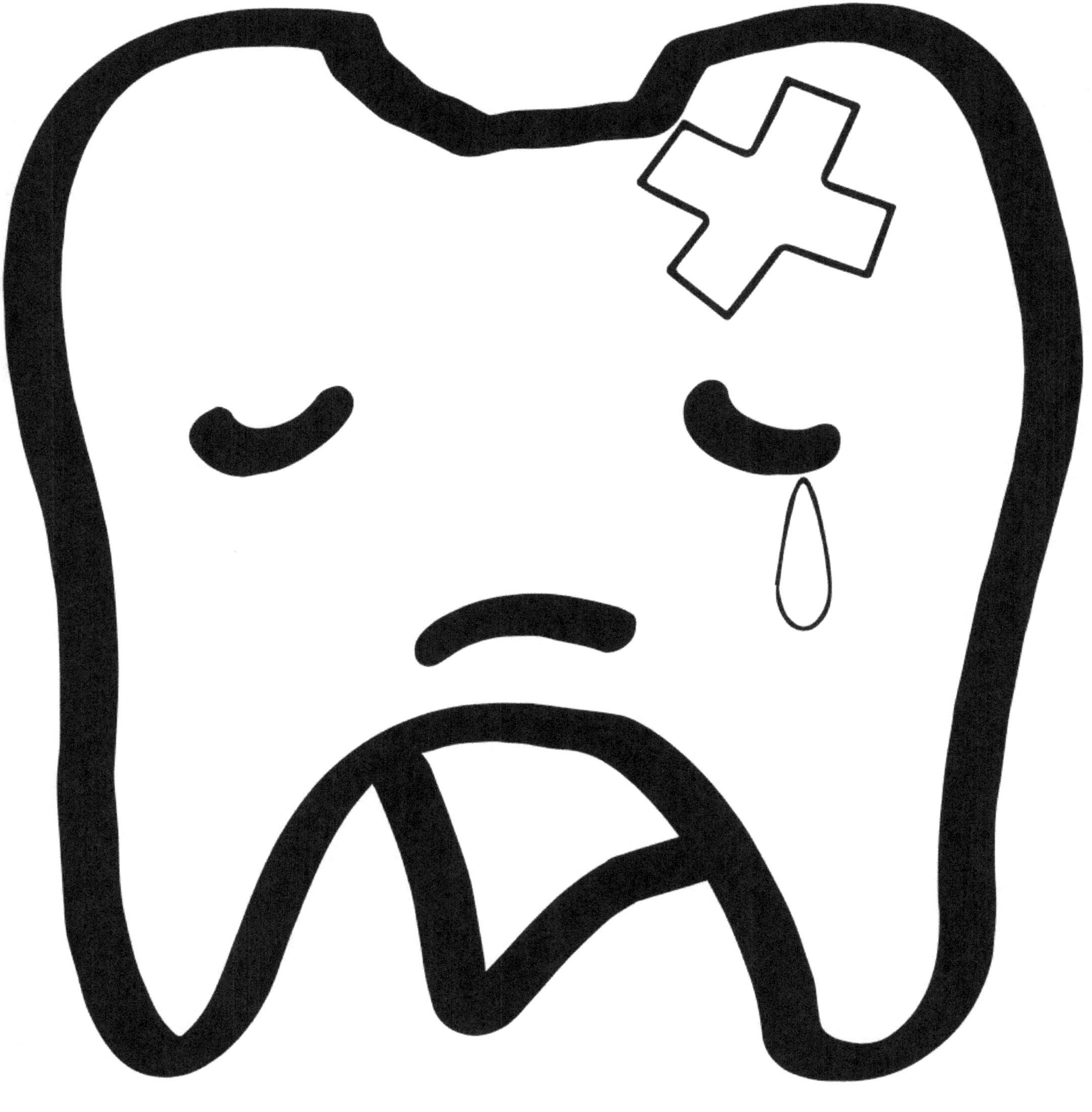

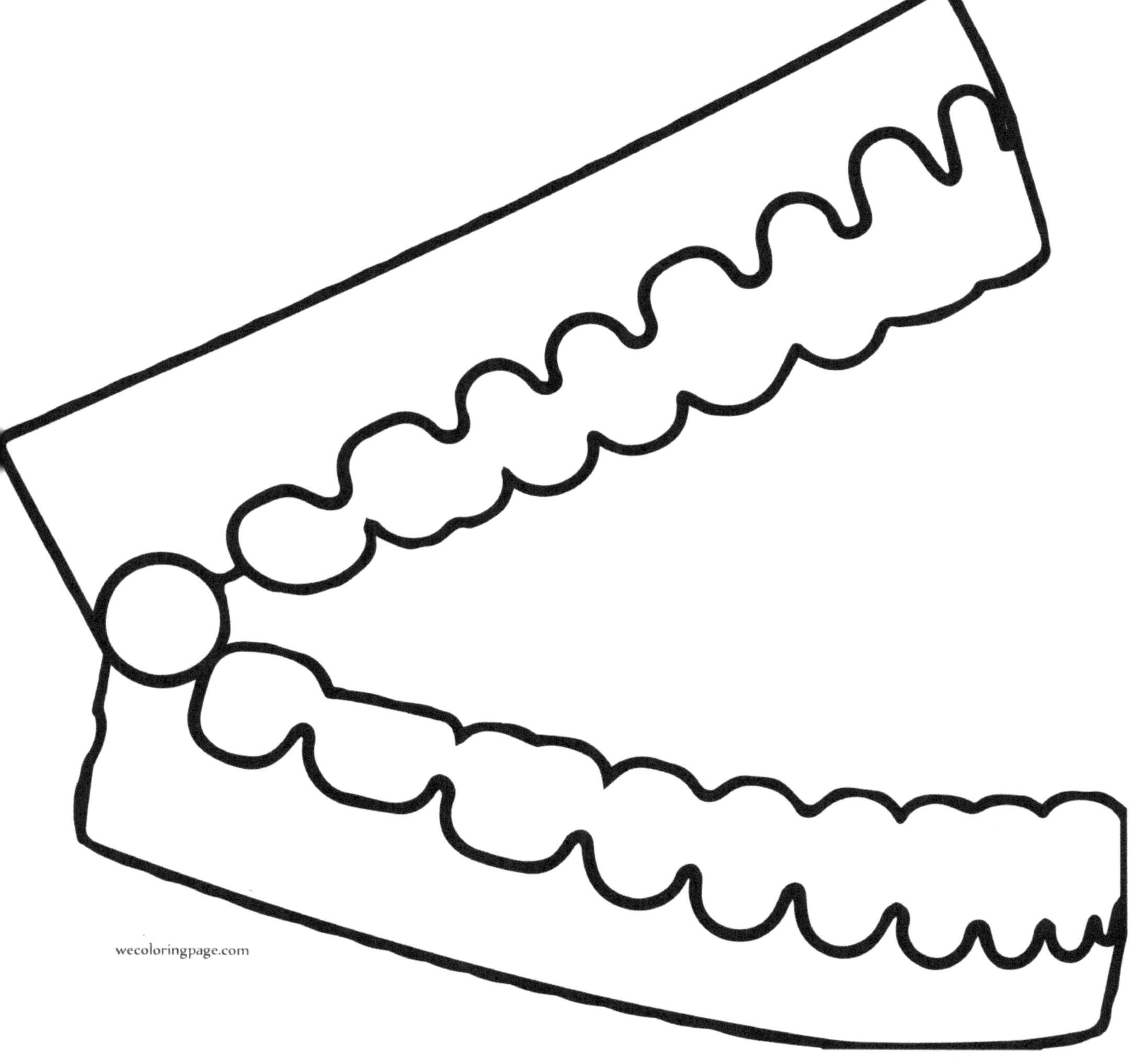

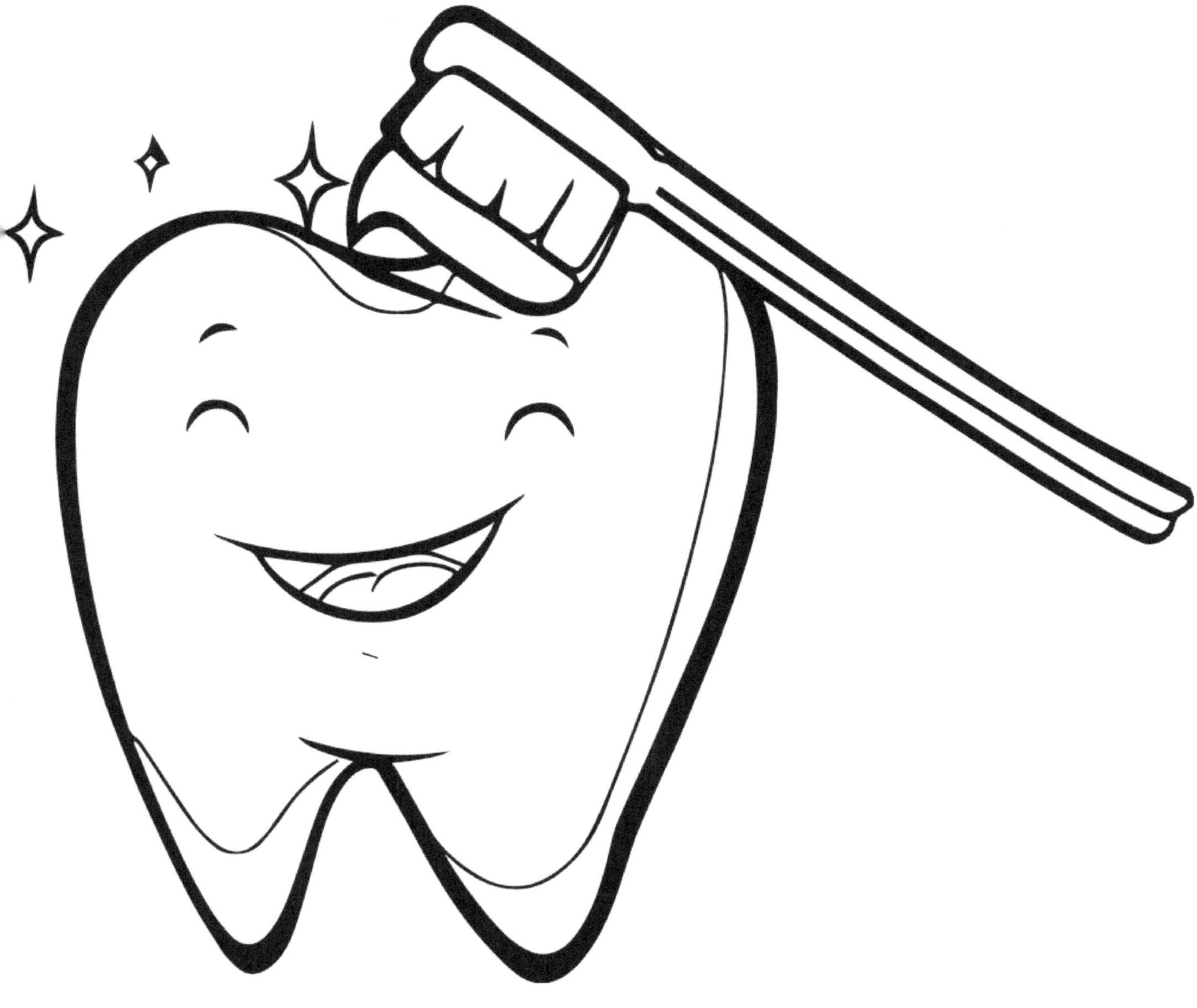

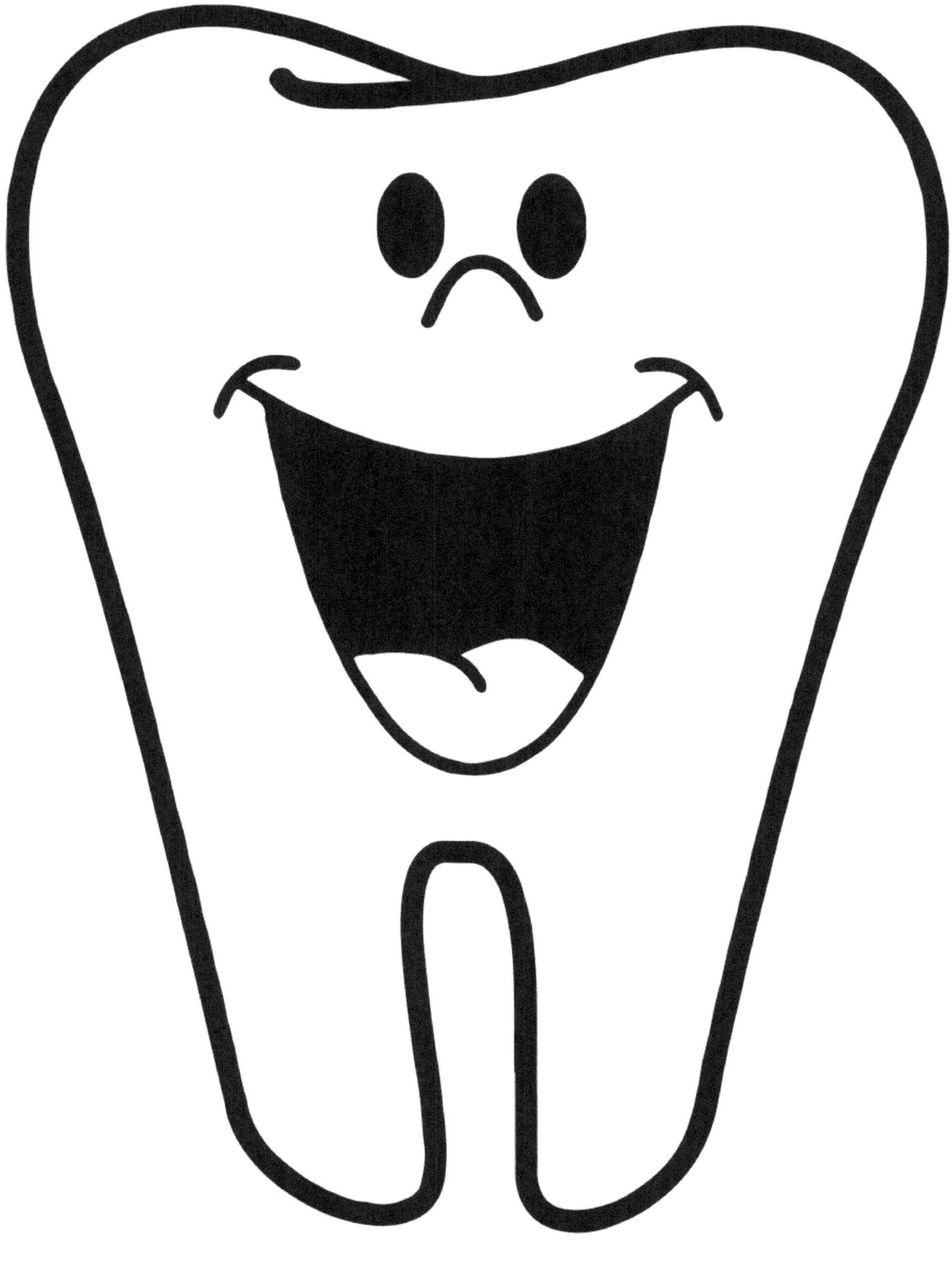

wecoloringpage.com

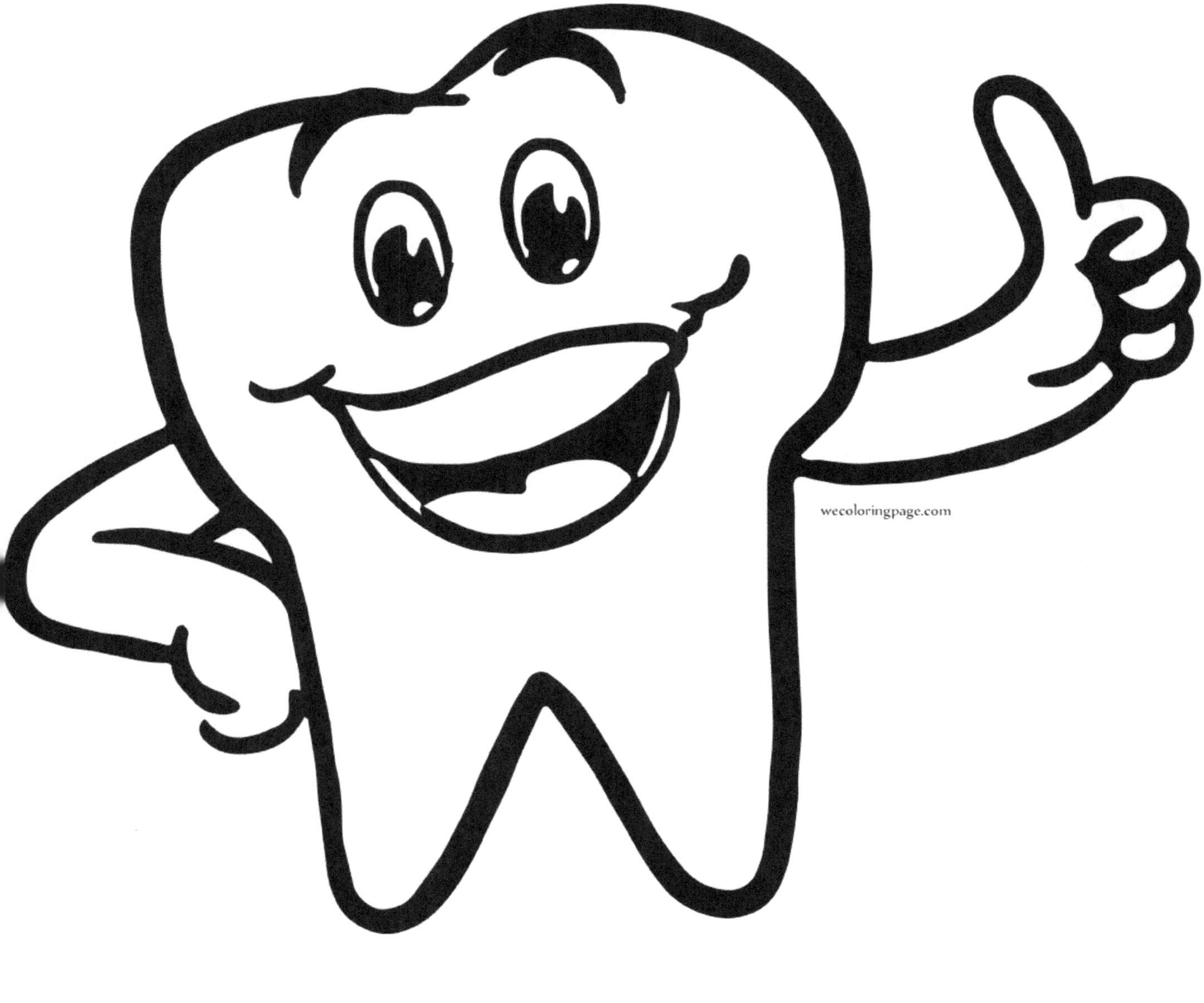

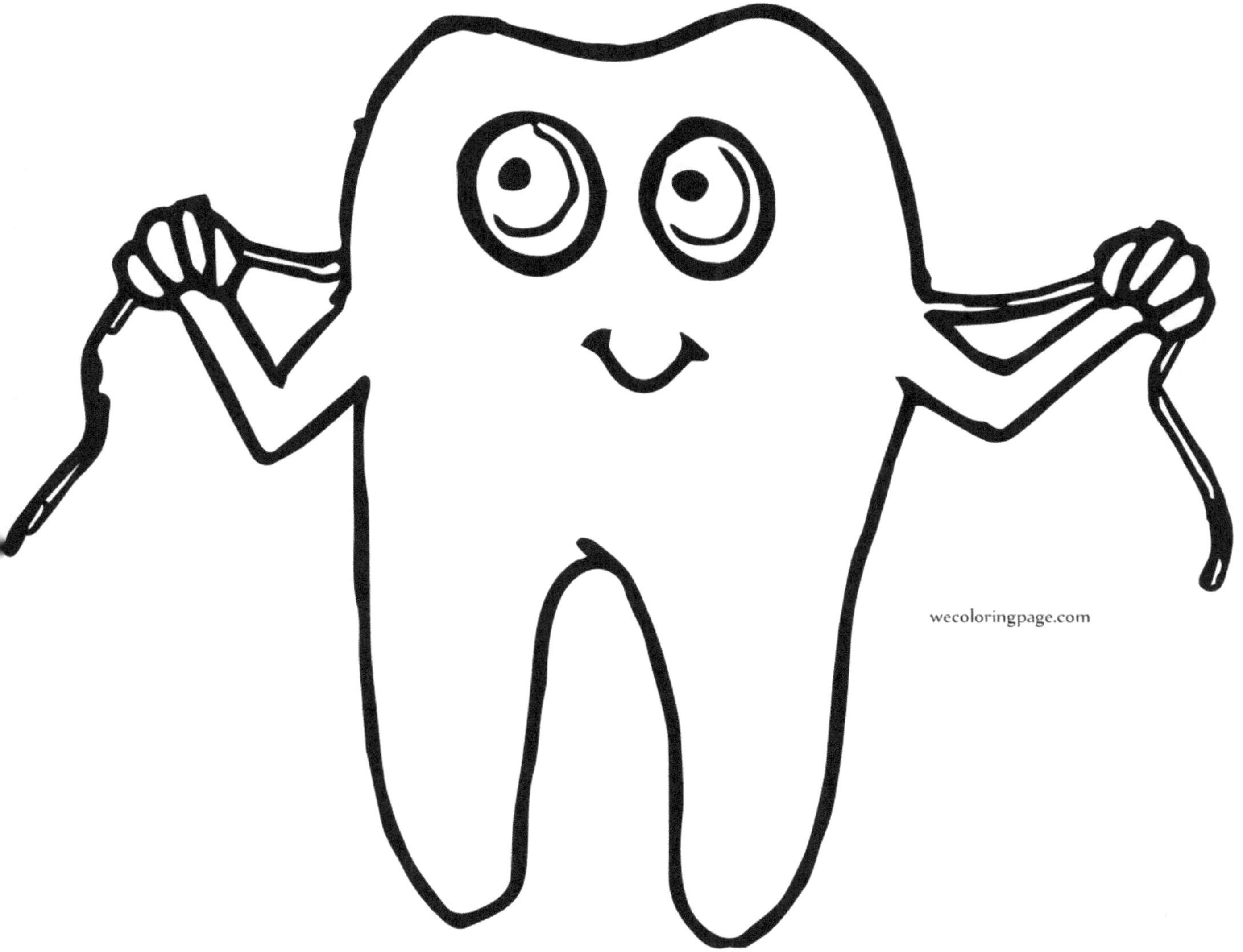

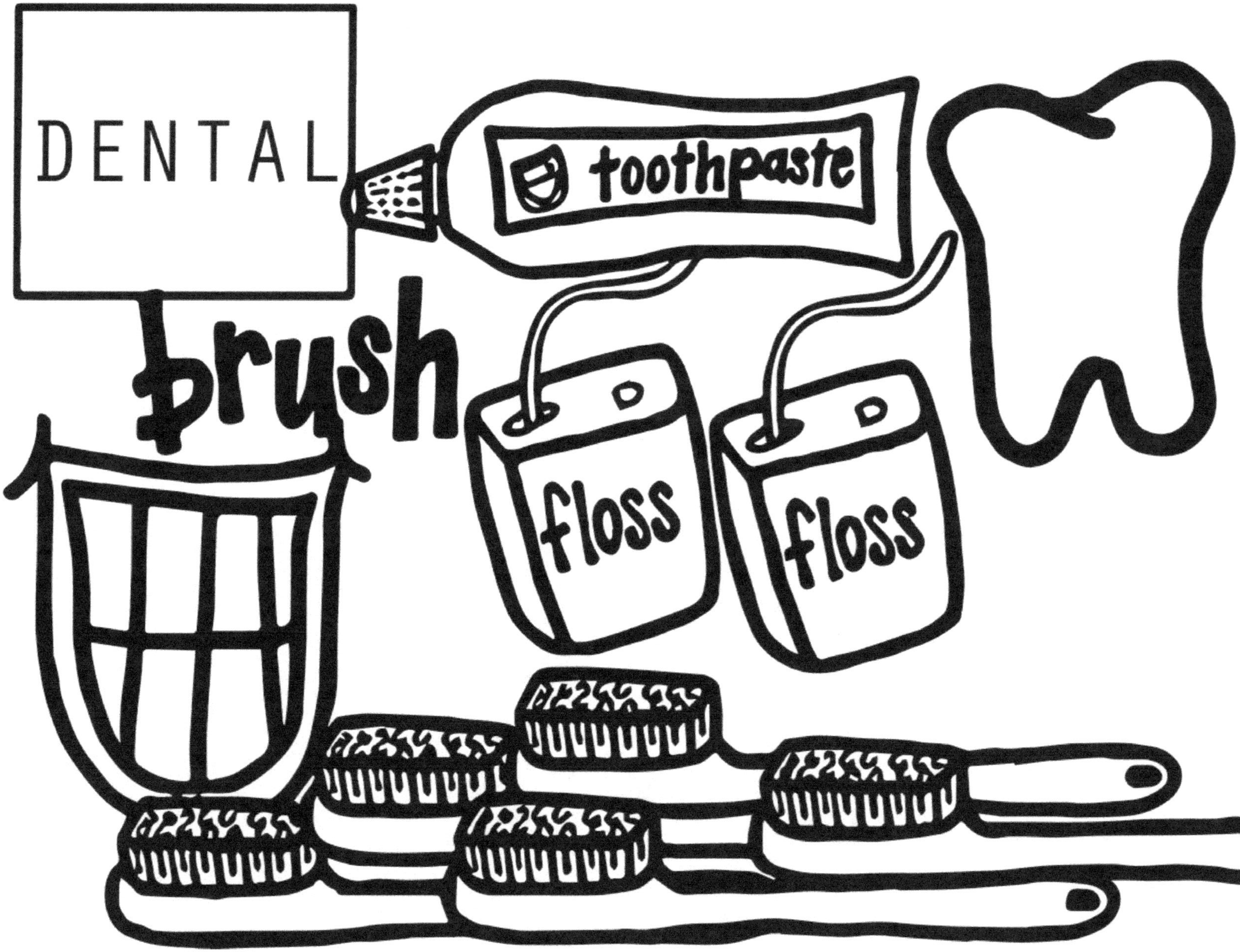
DENTAL
brush
toothpaste
floss
floss

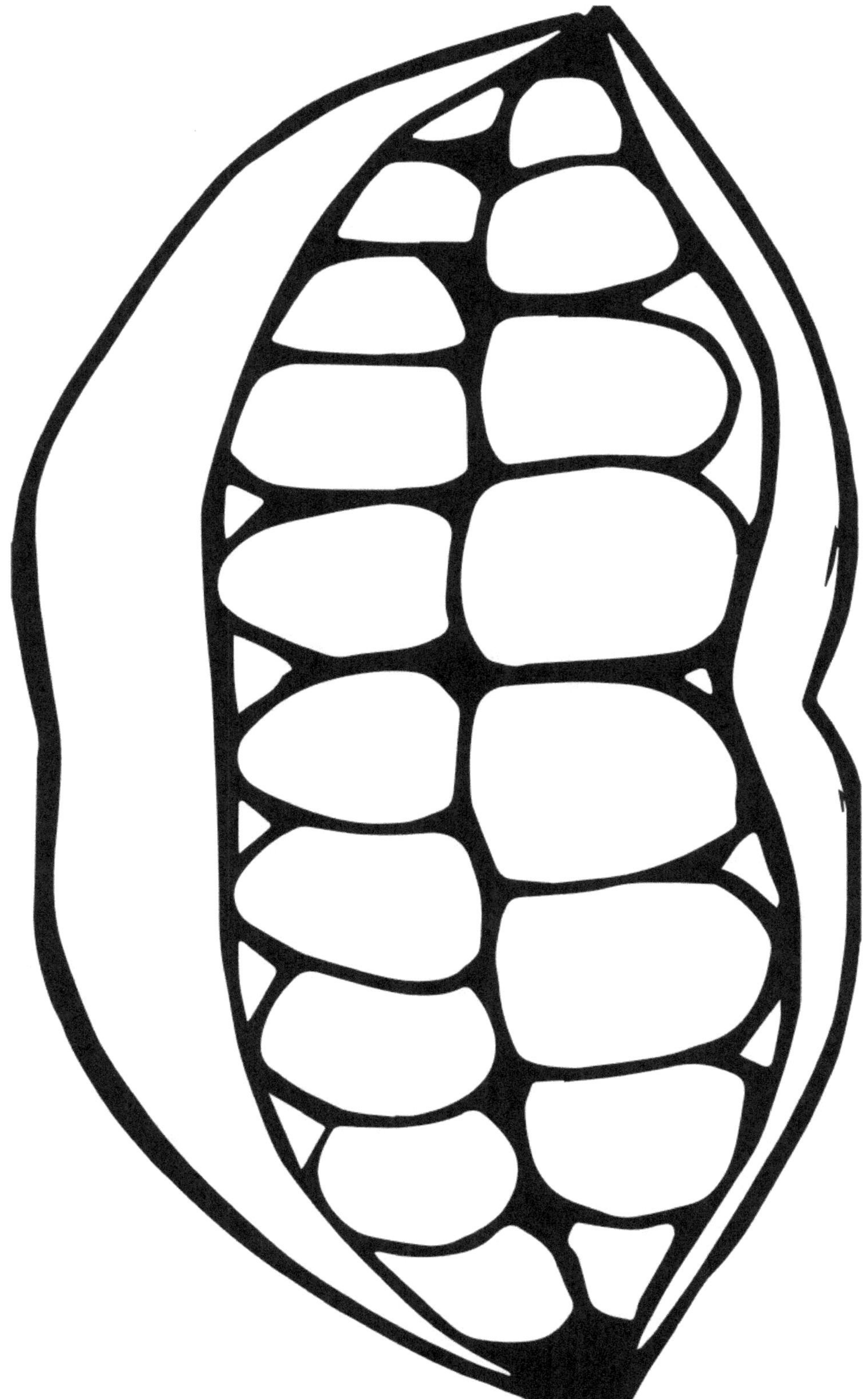

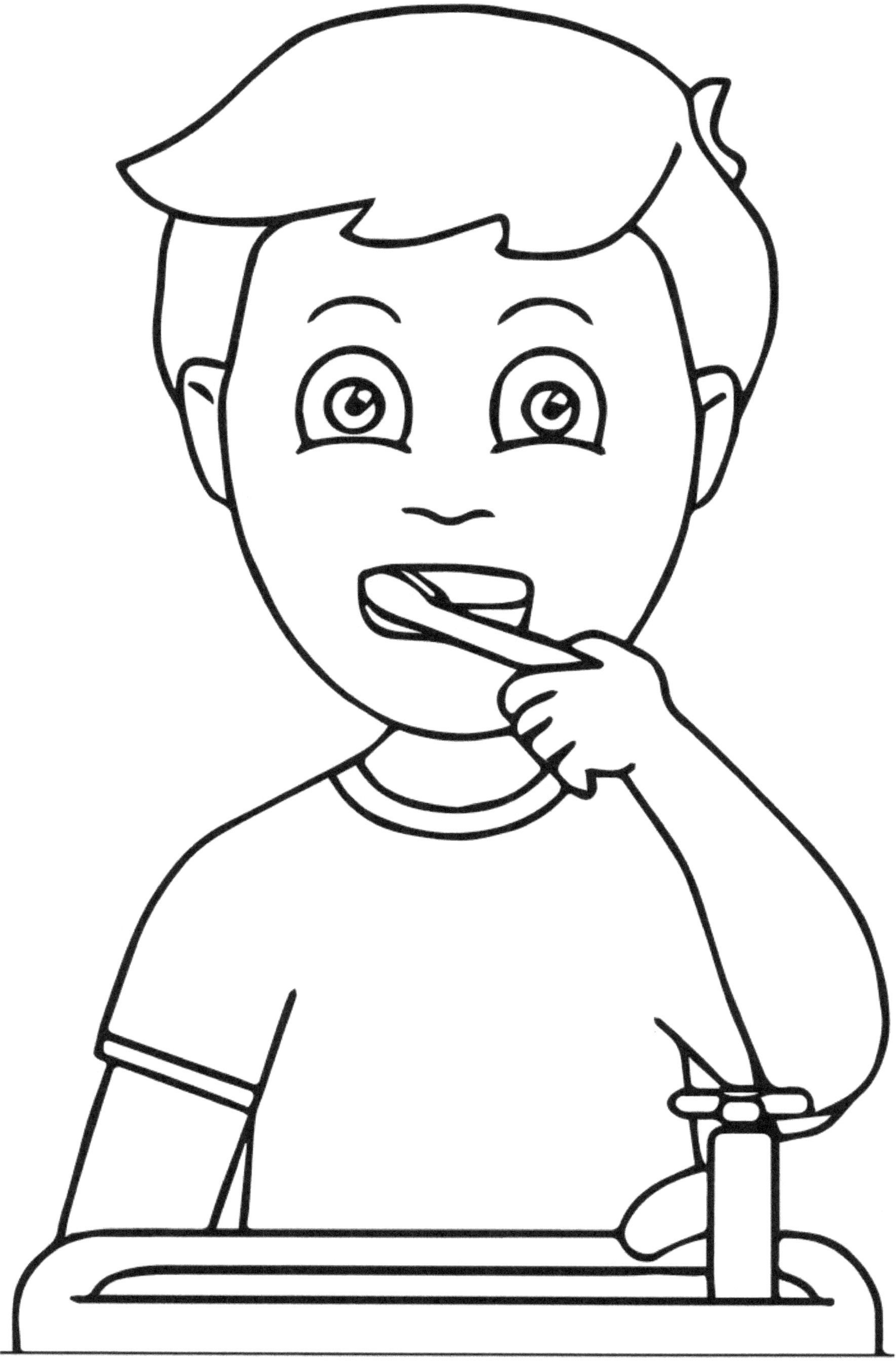

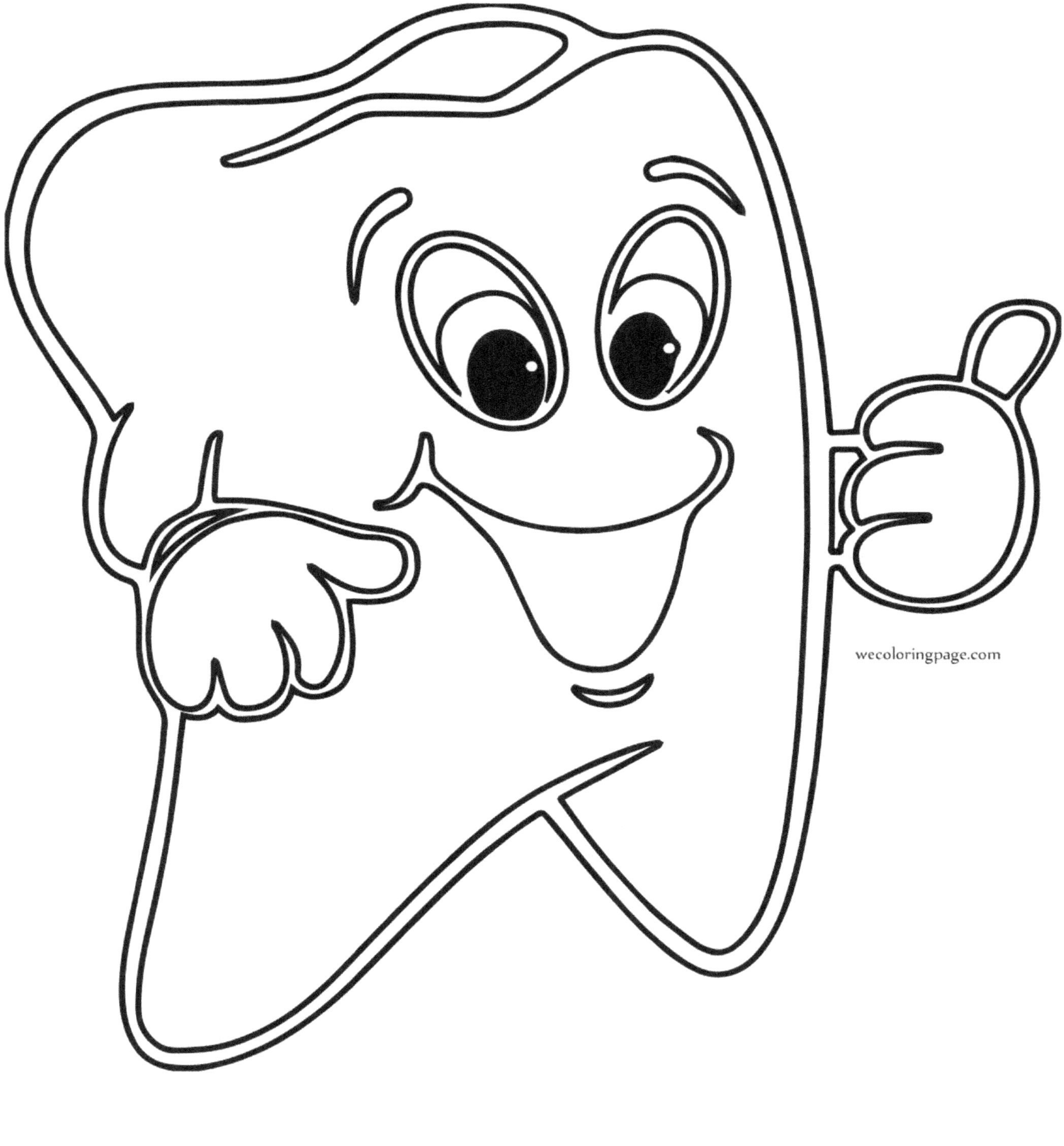

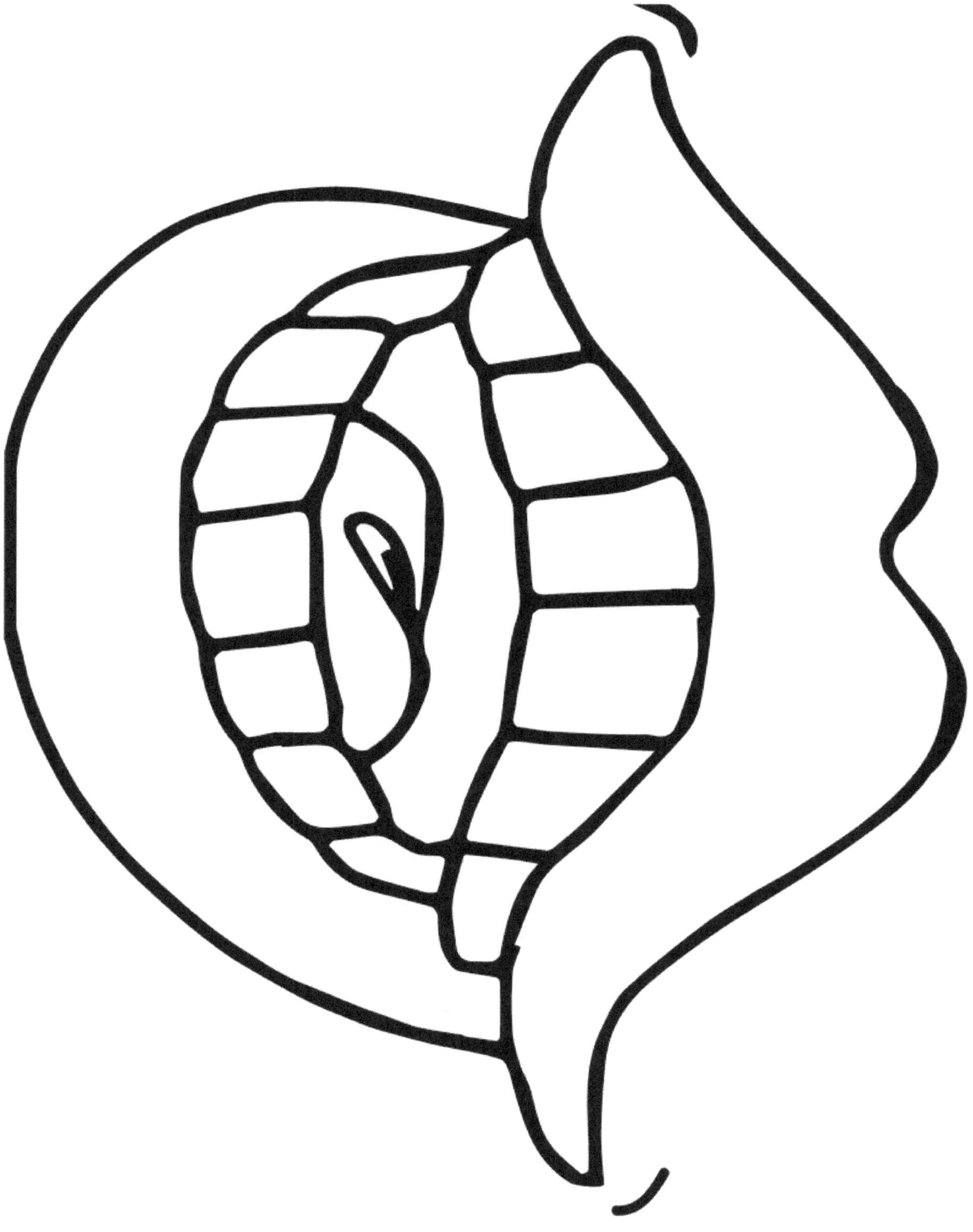

www.ingramcontent.com/pod-product-compliance
Lightning Source LLC
Chambersburg PA
CBHW081658220526
45466CB00009B/2798
* 9 7 8 1 6 8 7 2 6 9 7 1 3 *